Lucy Steckler is a Utah native, currently studying at Utah Valley University. She has always been an avid reader and writer, but did not begin writing poetry until serving as a missionary for the Church of Jesus Christ of Latter-Day Saints, sourcing inspiration from her experiences during that time.

To Grandma, a believer in hope.

Lucy Steckler

A WORD OF HOPE

AUSTIN MACAULEY PUBLISHERS™

LONDON • CAMBRIDGE • NEW YORK • SHARJAH

A CIP catalogue record for this title is available from the British Library.

ISBN 9781035825950 (Paperback)
ISBN 9781035825967 (ePub e-book)

www.austinmacauley.com

First Published 2023
Austin Macauley Publishers Ltd®
1 Canada Square
Canary Wharf
London
E14 5AA

HOPE TO HAVE

One raised up, who extended lift
To gather all — and fill
Hope to have, is His free gift
Remembered on a hill

With whole soul, a promise of abiding trust
In exchange — redemption
Offered in form of compassionate crust
Through merciful condescension

FLIP FLOP

Eyes open wider, no longer cast down,
Shoulders squared with every interaction,
Waves and smiles are no longer hesitant.
I'm new
I'm me
Confidence is a foreign language I speak fluently.

A nervous buzz in my stomach,
Has become fuel for my progression,
Obstacle has become welcome challenge.
It's freedom
It's strength
Assuredness graces my every move.

But tides will always change and mountains still end
in valleys. Confidence is not a constant. Like the
competence of language, it doesn't promise to remain
intact.
Practice helps, but consistent stumbling deems each
effort futile.
An erosive spiral ensues.

The grade seems bigger than the challenge.
Light, once plentiful, is scarce.

But tides will always change and valleys still engender mountains. Despair is not a constant. It comes and leaves empty spaces in its place, nothing left intact.
Spaces make room for the Savior's merciful love.
It's here that infinite grace abounds.

LADDERS

I like to think progress engenders confidence.
That it will make me comfortable.

But when life is a ladder
There is no cling of comfort,
No rung of respite.
And there is certainly no room and board for my
wearied efforts
Along those expectant beams.

A step of success is merely that —
A step, now behind.
Onto the next but keep in mind
To go forward or digress.
Choices, along a linear line.

HAPPY BIRTHDAY

Happy birthday,
Welcome to something brand new.

A celebratory commencement,
Of a journey designed just for you.

Here is a family, there are some friends.
Follow the spirit in all that you choose.

You're gifted with scripture, holy prophets too,
The blessings of Heaven promised if you will use.

Remember your past, hold to who you'll become,
Each chapter, a genesis, a legacy combined.

And so, begin each new journey with purpose:
To be like Him, a daughter divine.

I FELL IN LOVE WITH LIFE

I fell in love with life.
Cold and gray were my surroundings,
Until my eyes were opened to the golden rays of opportunity
Until my lungs began to breathe the freedom of existence
Until my ears were captivated by the majesty of music
Until my mind found the fascination of knowledge
Until I began to live.
Then, I fell in love with life.

KNOWING CHANGE

At a standstill
Comfortably trapped,
No longer ignorantly
Encaged.

Now I know,
What the ledge looks like
What the weight feels like
Why the urge sounds like

And yet
Knowing what I must do
I waver;
Searching for another way
A question similar to my Savior's
An answer much the same.

MY MOM

From the beginning I watched through brand-new eyes —
Building my world; she was sure to put the brightest light in the center.
This brought warmth, depth and life.
She taught me of sunshine.

Time went on, and clouds covered my sun.
I knew what sunshine was, but my skies remained dark.
As to not challenge the balance of nature, instead of raising the sun, she pointed out the stars.
She taught me to find light instead of waiting for it to appear.

Then, once my foundation was built by lessons of the heavens, we moved to study the Earth. Her life is many seasons, but she is a rock.
Epitome of strength and unmoving perseverance.
Though the winters are cold, she does not crack.

The heat of the summer burns, yet her surface remains cool.

Through rain and wind, still she stands.

Rain, sun or snow, she teaches me to endure.

And now, though distanced, still I learn.

Lessons of love and charity

She emanates consistent compassion; her ever sturdy rock is foundation and refuge to many.

Fearful and worried souls find solace in her sturdy perseverance.

She teaches me to serve selflessly, and to love others first.

God's plan is perfection, and so is my goal.

An example is provided, of what to become.

Not on my own, that cannot be done.

So, God sent me to this teacher, an angel,

Who I get to call Mom.

SEEKING JOY

Seeking happiness is picking flowers
Ephemeral beauty and satisfaction
Is quickly followed by withered leaves of unfulfilled
expectations
Even the brightest bouquet eventually fades.

Seeking joy is to draw from a well
Constant flow and reliability
Is independent of the drawer's bucket
Good and faithful is the supply, to be both are the
conditions.

GLASS CASTLE

Welcome to my fragile castle
Walk with trepidation, test every step
Listen for fractures and brace yourself

Be still and breathe soft
Be slow and stay steady
Walls of glass and sandy foundation
Require calculated motion

I long for soft carpeted floors
Steps that creak instead of fracture
I yearn for sturdy wooden beams
Doors that swing instead of shatter

Yet here I will stay and learn to be guarded
Careful to move, to speak, to think
Here I will wait and envy the sounds of freedom
Tuned in to wind, to rain,
To every creature outside my transparent walls.

POISONED BY HER PRESENCE

Here it is again, trickling its way in
Past the paper barricades, flimsy fortifications,
Coursing through paths already been.

To be so fragile!
To be poisoned by her presence.
To let the sickening serum coat each vein.
To trap a heart, once free to beat, in the pervasive solution.

But oh, how the Great Physician heals.

Here it is again, flowing gently through.
Clearing each vestige of infection,
Building slowly anew all defenses.

To be so free!
To be administered antidotal drink,
To be soothed by the balm of the book,
To taste the promised purification,
His word and His work complete.

HERE I AM

Here I am,
Languishing in a cerebral prison.
I have lost something most precious; my words.
What once held freedom in each thoughtful phrase,
Each a capsule of emotion, I lost.
Me, an empty captive to my own mind;
Prisoner of mental paralysis.
Walls I know I have put up on my own,
Yet I am powerless to choose again.

Here I am,
And where the pen fails, I wait on the Lord.
When ink and words run out, I turn to His.
He was the author, but now I'm the pen.
The words were never mine to write, but His.
They, which were so selfishly my freedom Become
the key to someone else's chain
An instrument in His hands I will be —
Lord wherever you need me, here I am.

CONFIDENCE AND COMPARISONS

You stand in the center of a deep, green wood.
Surrounded by paths to take, you wonder which you should.

A voice says to choose, move forward with confidence.
With nothing to lose, a step taken, no fear of recompense.

Through the trees you see others, also on their own.
Traveling on avenues along which they've grown.

Separate they roam, yet united in cause.
A whisper is felt, a quiet pause.

Though your lonesome can feel heavy,
You should know that there are many.

Many paths to take and ways to wander,
Though other seem short while yours always longer.

Each road that you choose is meant for you,
So do not compare, only continue.

You are not alone, and neither are they,
Have confidence. Persevere. Come what may.

JUST BE

What is there when I approach the wall?
       Stillness of uncertainty.

Brittle serenity, where stony faces stand tall,
       I'm reminded to just be.

Here I stand when I buckle, I begin to break
       Prickled fear grows.

It's all too much, I start to shake
       A whisper says someone else knows.

Engraved and outstretched, his hand awaits
       His loving assurance is heard.

I don't understand until He restates,
       "Lay hold upon my word."

We've started our climb, the slow ascent
       Yet familiar stones remind of where I fell.

I feel weak, the wall I now resent
        His counsel to me, "Endure it well."

With perfect understanding of my plight
        Down falls a saving cord.

When my next handhold is out of sight,
        I know I can inquire of the Lord.

Nearing the top, still He's with me
        Salvation and comfort bought.

The weight of walls to come rests heavy
        He reminds again, "Fear not."

RESOLUTION

Why can't I think myself into resolution?
Even the endless expanse whispers promises of purpose.
Yet the stars, I have found,
Yield no answers.

I'm left to wander, to wonder what's next,
Chasing the elusive verdict of my ever-questioning thoughts.
Nothing makes sense, and I cannot decide.
This space in my mind, that I love;
A forlorn prison, condemned to reside.

But it's comfortable here, or maybe just familiar.
Does the difference really matter,
If my shackles leave no bruise?
I could search for hours but all I would ever find
Is us here under a twinkling blanket, soon to be sunrise.

BEST OF THE BEST

The best of the best,
And they are mine.

On account of wonderful gospel,
Forever and for time.

My people, my friends,
Always they will be.

Oh Lord, I am grateful for your gift,
Beautiful eternity.

ALL FOR YOU

Tears I cry, and words I write,
      They're all for you.

Memories fray as I lose sight,
      Of times it was us two.

The aching hurt and golden happy,
      Inextricably tied.

It's bittersweet, forgetting;
      Ignoring the hole inside.

A WAIT

Inside me sits a weight.
With it, I sink
Each day another leaden drop builds
My collection of despair

With trust that he hears, hope for days without tears
I pray with faith for this weight to be rid
The response to my pleas, His council to my cries
Is wait.

For better days, a change of life. For the promises
He's made.
"Have faith," he teaches,
"My sacrifice, a gift
Believe in me and persevere,
You are promised merciful lift."

And so, I wait on the Lord.
I begin to see, to understand.
Long ago a weight was carried,
Much heavier than mine.

In a garden, on a hill, in a tomb buried;
My brother's path you will find.
The weight of all others,
Even this weight of mine
He humbly and nobly bore
So, when the burden consumes
And everything is heavy
I am assured it's been endured before.

With my relief found, the world is bathed in new light
With empathetic lenses I look around.
My friends and His children —
I watch them shoulder a weight they carry alone.
My heart breaks for I know a better way,
One of hope and healing, one that to me has been
shown.

Their weight is too heavy as I ask, "Lord what will you
do?"
Gently he reminds me, "Daughter, I have sent them
you."
So, the message I bring is not mine
Love, and hope, and ease are His to give
Your part to play is trust and time

The times that I struggled, the times that we cried
Have opened our eyes to grace,
softened our hearts to change.

Our conversion to Him — solidified.
We have learned of His goodness and experience has taught,
Eternal bliss is worth the weight.

SHE IS

There we were, all circled up.
Our words, mere footsteps in the past.
Each voice offered a cherished memory —
One that to all could relate.
But something was wrong.

Mixed into memories of days and years gone by was
the present —
The present her.
How subtle the tragedy of who she was —
Juxtaposed with who she is.

Though those moments solely in our minds remain,
to this day her person still prevails.
When I speak of her, I am careful to speak of who I
love, not who I loved.
I don't remember who she was, rather who she is
today.
I do not mourn the loss of that which I know still is.

SAVIOR

Savior of mine, a Savior indeed.
More than all else, that's who He is to me.
But as experience teaches, I've come to know,
That to me and many, He is more.

A word of encouragement,
An ideal of resilience
So much He so freely gives;
We call Him Hope.

A shattered heart mended,
A rogue tear dried
It is He who makes all things right;
We call Him Physician.

From a fallen state,
A vagrant being
He lifts, saves and makes new;
We call Him Redemption

A captive that He frees
An army that He leads
Subject to Him, so merciful, just and wise;
We call Him King.

THE PIT

Talking to you is like joining you in the pit you've fallen into.

It's so dark, and it's so deep and you are completely hopeless.

I sit and listen.

I feel it when you crumble, I watch as you fall even farther down.

But footsteps are in the distance.

A dull light appears.

Encouraging words fall on boarded up ears.

He approaches and extends His hand. You just have to take it, forget your fears. "Come," He pleads.

His merciful gift, though to you is free,

Paid your way out of this pit

And opened doors to eternity.

But my love, you have to choose and you have to trust.

I will stay with you here, and so will He.

But what's just beyond the threshold is soulful liberty.

DANGERS OF A WANDERING MIND

The dangers of a wandering mind are real.

Tempting whispers of memories will lure one into thought's abandoned corners. There to waste away with moments already lived.

Cunning chatter of intelligence threatens another with false philosophy's cold edge. There the attractive blade cuts apart conviction.

Persuasive voices of distorted reality destroy the very mind itself. There, the mirror of self-perception is shattered.

So do not wander, but seek wonder to tame.
With trepidation tread and be warned; the dangers of a wandering mind are real.

A FEAR

It started in my toes.
They became the fragile stone that built my fear to walk.
One wrong move, one small bump, and I begin to crumble.

The stiffness spread and trapped my legs.
They are the physical counterpart to my fear paralysis.
If I move, if I walk, I know that I would break.

The disease eventually encases me.
My protective stillness betrays, becoming the enablement of the sickness' journey.
I am frozen, I am fragile, I live in fear.

I've become something unable to bend, unable to change,
Trapped inside this stone.

It is a curse I brought on myself. The idyllic future I so rigidly clung to became the immovable walls I could never escape.

The stone prison of my resistance to change is now the reason I never will.

All that is left, all that is free
Is the rubble of my message.
Don't do the same as I did.
Sometimes, to break the fragile growth is the only way to build,
And the only way to live free.

BROKEN

I came to visit after some time away.
Past the warm and familiar door,
I was met with the remnant shards
Of you, my family.

The haunting panes, once part of a whole,
Reflect at times, days that are past.

My heart follows suit.
It's broken.
The pieces of you cut at my core
Before continuing their crumble.

"Stop," I plead.
"Please let me help you."
But my cries are in vain as I watch
What once was beautiful,
Become unrecognizable.
Become broken.

MY COLLECTION

I collect my hardships as they come, like putting solemn stones in a bag.

Each rock, or even pebble, is a weight.
Laden with painful memories and precious lessons, I keep them close.

While grief is the burden of the boulder, healing is not the removing of such from my bag.

Healing is found in the holding of each stone —
And in remembering those heavy moments.

It is found in knowing that they are yours —
Your weight, your worry and your wings.

Who would you be without them?
One without the weight to withstand the storms of life.
One without an immovable and hard-won foundation.

One too afraid to collect stones down a future path to remind you of where you've been.
One who abandons the past when the memory is too much to carry on.

Grief does not erode, it layers. It comes, it stays, it settles.
Pain does not subside, it lingers. It strengthens, builds, and reminds.

This path that we call life will fill your bag.
Carry on, continue, and collect.
These weighty stones have built your person.
And what you have built together is what you will leave behind.

WORDS OF COMFORT

These are for you
When you feel down
Words of comfort from one broken but beating heart
to another.

Are you lonely?
Know that He was too
So, God sent an angel, just as He sent a Savior for you.

Are you without hope?
Know that there is light to be found
He came out from the tomb and all will come up from
the ground.

Are you waiting?
Waiting on the Lord is trusting
In His time, His goodness and His blessings.

Are you wondering?
If you're His child, if He hears?
You are.

He does.
The desire of your heart falls on listening ears.

I know you hurt
And no, these words are not new.
Simple truths, nothing grandiose
But these you must know, for they mean the most.

JUST DIFFERENT

It's not difficult, just different.
It may not fill the box you built.
But maybe vestigiality is your invitation
To leave it.

Think for a moment,
Breathe in the minute.
From another to the next,
No one is the same.

Embrace the change,
With it comes self-discovery.
The pattern of progression;
A dynamic process.

And so remember
While life carries waves of change,
The ebbs and flows are neither wholly good nor bad.
It's not difficult, just different.

HIS NAME

I'm in His hands and watchful care.
He is on my heart, His name I wear.

By this I am called, His work I will do.
As representative and missionary too.

Whatever the task or who I must be.
Now and always. Savior, you have me.

THE PICTURE OF POWER

The picture of power,
>Standing aglow
>Declaring truth hard won.

The statement of truth,
>Solid in conviction
>Born of sacrifice and tribulation.

The promise of blessings,
>Sincerely expressed
>Earnestly hoping they will receive.

The plea of love,
>Extended in faith
>Accounted to self, to Him, and His Son.

THE SEARCH

He sees His children searching
      As he watches from his throne above,
His heart is saddened greatly
      By a world without love.

His sons, and His daughters
      Desperate and starved of His word.
Choose shallow books dearth of wisdom
      To His, incomprehensibly preferred.

How His heart must ache to see the sick,
      Preyed upon by all evils combined.
So, One He sent to heal
      The bruised, the bleeding and the blind.

This One, even the way,
      The truth and the light.
Calls others to the field of harvest,
      To labor with all their might.

Find His children, feed lost sheep
        To each corner and clime, they're sent.
Side by side with the Physician himself,
        Inviting all to change and to repent.

In taking a closer look,
        One might be surprised.
That these people who struggle,
        Are more than their burdens in God's eyes.

This one here has lost touch,
        With his heavenly roots and veiled past.
To Him is administered pure truth
        Supernal potential, no longer an outcast

And her, this daughter of a king,
        Is consumed by snares of comparison.
To her is shown a careful exemplar
        Whose path she follows from that prison.

There're others, wayward children
        Who fight the battle of addiction.
It's them He will free, it's for them
        He suffered — even their self-affliction.

This is why we search,

      And this is why we find.

To declare to them a Savior,

      Of just to them, and to all mankind.

SACRED TIME

Sacred time, the still and quiet.
Where thoughts are more.
I find clarity, security and order in those
contemplative moments.

The steady drip of consciousness flows through my
day.
But to ponder is to draw from a well.
There is value in each fleeting thought, though the
ones that stay are treasures.

OBEDIENCE

To each the laws of heaven are given,
The first of them all, obedience.
What seems to be rigid, restrictive and rote
Is the guardrail to power, and liberty's key.
What seems a dictation, a demand, and a duty
Is the instruction of growing love, faith, and
character.

Not even He, a king, exempt.
Though perfect, still He scouted our path of
imperfect mortality
Submissive to the Father, He set for all the pattern of
submission.
To all is promised,
Freedom, upon faith to obey
Knowledge, beautifully earned.
Power, submissively won
Protection, through loyalty bestowed.
Life eternal, by capitulation of one's will.

MY JESUS

Hello old friend, it's me again.
It's been a while since we've spoken.
Things got messy when I left. The other day —
I saw your name; I took it for a sign

So, hey. How are you?
The same I've been told.
The one "who does not change", "who always stays".
And me? Yeah, I'm fine.

I guess I just got lost,
I may have made some bad decisions.
You said before, you knew the way?
Maybe you could offer some advice.

You see life is darker for me now,
It's hard to make out the path.
The world has left a few stains on me.
But I think I'm ready now, and some council would be
nice.

Hmmm, I like that.
Trusting you is easy enough.
A plan you say? I could use the step by step.
Friend, please, tell me more of what I must do.

I think I can do this!
You'll stay with me, right?
It says here, right in your book that you will.
You'll walk with me, and I'll walk with you.

That worked for a minute, things were good!
But oh, I'm embarrassed to say it —
I know you showed me the way,
Though I've made some mistakes.

This time I need more than words.
I see it clearly, your outstretched arm.
How is it that you are so good?
The guilt I feel, your compassion abates.

You're a true friend, you know.
A confidant.
Consistent, trustworthy, reliable.
But it is your love that I will never comprehend and
forever strive to have.
Thank you, dear friend. For all you've been for me.
More than a friend, but a Redeemer, Lord and King.

WHAT I SEE

What I have envisioned is walls of white.
A family built with gospel ties.

I can see in my mind – a temple.
A sanctuary, a safe space, a sense of security.

I picture us together.
We are closely knit, one with another and one in Christ.

My family, I pray, is eternal.
What I see goes beyond a parted veil, I glimpse light that lasts forever.

Printed in the USA
CPSIA information can be obtained
at www.ICGtesting.com
LVHW021749200923
758649LV00062B/1343